ACKNOWLEDGEMENTS

Acknowledgements are due to the editors of *Dreamcatcher* magazine, *Bittersweet Embrace* (website) and the anthology *London Noir* (Akashic Books, USA) where some of these pieces were first published. 'Bradford' was originally commissioned by Bradford City Council, 'Fortune Favours the Tattooed Heart' by Yorkshire Museum Services, 'Talisman' by The Captain Cook Memorial Museum, Whitby, and 'So Many Names are Lost Now' by The Royal Armouries, Leeds.

First published in Great Britain in 2006 by Comma Poetry
Comma Press, 3 Vale Bower, Mytholmroyd, West Yorkshire HX7 5EP
www.commapress.co.uk
Distributed by Inpress
www.inpressbooks.co.uk

The publishers gratefully acknowledge assistance from the Arts Council England North West, and the Regional Arts Lottery Programme, as well as the support of Literature Northwest, which is itself assisted by ACE NW and CIDS (The Creative Industries Development Service), Manchester.

· Set in Bembo by Comma Press.

pray for us sinners

JOOLZ DENBY

For Justin Sullivan &
Michael Davis:
my respect and gratitude to
the Goddess, as ever.

CONTENTS

Boy, you need the Road

Boy, you need the Road;
the lazy white stitch of heaven's path leading through the
sun's bright benediction criss-cross and mazy to some
wild-thyme scented hillside lying silvery sweet and
blood warm under high cirrus clouds embroidering
the lapis-lazuli of the southern sky like prayer flags,
far, far away from the bricks and mortar menagerie
of your home town's crash-and-burn Saturday night circus.

Boy, you need the Road;
nights of fast-forward spirit-driven dazzling highs;
luminous surf pulse of breathing icy turquoise oceans,
you sprawled on a black beach wrapped in a ragged blanket,
a salt-green witch fire flickering cold and lighting up no earthly place
but burning in your flesh like those lost and long-gone kisses you
miss so much and crave with a junkie's jack-up fever
in your aching and unmended heart.

Boy, you need the Road;
playing your old guitar through dawn's blue incense
that rises over canyons of crystal sheathed skyscrapers
in a hotel room so bleach-clean and anonymous it hurts;
the songs you pick so idly the diary of your flight;
staring into the lying whore of a mirror that shows a face you
would not have known to be your own – a face that shows everything
but tells nothing to the world you travel like a cruel angel.

Boy, you need the Road;
it will be your sweet and savage consolation, Star;
it will be your demon lover and your loving mother both,
wrapping you in webs of contradiction and razor-bright illusion,
as sinning saint and sanctified sinner you eat magic, breathe voodoo,
try everything as you search through souks and shanties, plazas
and favellas – dirt and diamond-crusted alike – for a way
into the shadow-land to find your true name and your dead love.

1

Boy, you need the Road;
if you don't go, go, go – fast as those great opal wings can bear you
out of the stink and ceremony of your expected life -
if you don't go – and this is no word of a lie, my sweetheart,
real life will get you, and a nice girl and her babies
will get you and bang-up straight-time work will get you
and you'll choke on it all in the neat little chain-store bedroom
where you cry when you think no one hears your terrible pain.

Boy, you need the Road;
better run, baby, better run right now and don't look back
because you mustn't regret and you mustn't hear the siren song
sung by the ones who stayed and lost and drank and drugged
their way to their own safe and stinking seat at the bar in Hell Town:
so run fast on those long legs and shake the clinging dust
of home from your boot heels as an offering to Holy Mother Mary,
a sacrifice for your last chance free and clear rock n' roll great escape.

Well, that's my prayer for you, anyhow; that's my last blessing.

So, boy; you need the Road;
you need the Road,
you need the Road,
Boy listen, listen, listen – before it's all too late.

You need the Road.

Cradle to Grave

Out of the split shank blood-dappled flesh
of our mothers, coasting the short ride to earth
in a slime wet-suit to the pulse of the expulsion tango
we hit air – breathe – hit air – howl with half
inflated lungs and a hand slaps us into being
hung upside down in a tangle of connections and
twisting to the staccato gulp and catch of
Mama trying to understand the becoming of us;

We know the rules but we won't obey 'em.

Do this, be this, it's wrong, it's right – the wickering
picket fence of regulation corrals us tighter
than a hobbled horse as we turn, turn and turn again
in nose-to-arse circles trying to devise our best
laid plan of escape while we still have time, while time
has us in his green grasp and we watch the cool
and ever-darkening red horizon of finality
with something approaching insanity;

We know the rules but we won't obey 'em.

Why should we? Answer us this simple question,
give us a clever and a cogent argument,
thrill us with your acumen, Agent Starling, do;
make us see the crystal beauty of your bright reasoning
and convince us that it's all for our own good
but be quick, be quick, for rapidly we run out of
patience, we run out of smiles, we run out of courtesy
we just want to run and run and run;

We know the rules but we won't obey 'em

Well, damn us, the already damned, if you seem
tongue-tied and twisted – can it be you're not so clever
after all? Can it be the brute evidence of why we shouldn't
far outweighs the why we should? The clack-yattering

of pundits and politicians winding up on coke and whiskey
preaching abstinence and prudence as a whore in cheap-jack
sex-clothes picks their pockets and tattles to the Sun;
kiss and tell, oh, tell me and kiss me, because so far you're wrong;

We know the rules and we won't obey 'em.

We would re-make and re-take the short wild ride
that's our life, that's our one life, that's our only
bang-up hard-won heaven – we know the brevity of what we have
and in the cracking seam of dawn as we fight for oxygen
again just like that first amniotic choke
we've got to – oh, come on you've got to – wonder why we tolerate
the robber barons and the call to prayers;
the bells and sorry kow-tow that ribs our days in a
trussed tight strain of claustrophobic tussling
while the zombie government elites bomb their
way to money, the brute kick of power and eternal infamy

and then – get this brethren and sisteren – tell us the how and
why and should and shouldn't of our precious being on this precious
earth.

Moral certitude. You got to love that, right?

Aw, fuck it.

So yeah, we know the rules, we really do, but you know what?

We won't obey 'em.

Hope

A poem for Thornbury Primary School

What we take from here is more than we can ever give back;
word-embroidered, book-learned, the great still music of numbers;
stories and poetry – the unending romance and magic of the world
laid flat on our desks in a map, countries patchworked out of the sea
in a raggled quilt of distance and dreaming.

We can give back as a gift only the bright pattern of our lives.

Playing, we run shouting nothing but the huge energy of childhood,
like an ancient song whose refrain is echoed in the tall city trees
that thread our terraced streets and the cool sweeps of rough grass
dotted with ponies, carved through by railways and bound by stone
walls;
we are all of us caught under the high bright cloud-veiled Northern
sky.

Some of us were heroes, some mothers, some scholars, all illuminated.

We remember the voices of our teachers as the years pass,
we tell our children what we were told; we hear them
tell their children and so the great chain turns, link after link.
We came to this place from every part of the spinning globe
and our voices are a living tapestry woven on Bradford looms.

We went into the world and we were proud of our home, and our
beginnings.

This place, this school, this new house of Life is *hope*,
each of us holding hope and the future in our hearts
like a jewel; each of us standing straight and breathing deep,
knowing if we falter, if the way is hard, we have that
precious shining thing to steady us and guide us on.

We sing one song, we tell one story: Together now, and ever.

In The Blood

My mother talked to me the other day about my grandfather;
usually, she doesn't care to talk much about the past,
having left it behind her as fast as she could run.
Like a child who broke a vase or tore her dress,
she prefers not to remember things she did.

But in the rusty iron cold of a late autumn day
she said, without warning, in the middle of another conversation,
that I had been her father's favourite.
Did I remember? Did I remember waiting
for him to come home when I was very small,
impatiently standing by the door,
when the afternoon turned slowly to dusk and I knew,
without the knowledge of clocks, it was time.

I would run out to him as soon as he opened the gate;
he would catch me up and swing me into the air,
laughing, then carry me indoors.
Did I remember? Did I remember how he would
pick me up out of bed at night when I woke and was afraid
and sing softly as he walked around the room with me
in his arms; he never did that for her, she said,
when *she* was a baby, and her face closed against memories.

But I don't remember my grandfather.
The journey has been long and hard and I smell winter in the air.
I don't remember – but I have a feeling, physical, unreasonable,
that seems to see the image of him,
melancholy and out of step with the marching world,
dark eyes gazing at horizons whose distances he finally reached
when his congested heart clenched into a savage fist
and ceased to beat; ceased to be the rhythm that
bought me safe back to sleep and quiet dreams.

I don't remember; but my own heart,
sharing his ruined blood, won't forget.

The Spirit House

The room my grandmother walked in was filled with
the spirits of the dead; round her they coiled and tumbled,
fluttering in ragged opalescent transparencies their faces
worn thin and dumb by distance, time and their smoky
impossible existence in the house of the living.

Watching her watching them in the fat crackling firelight,
hearing her breathing in the old bed next to mine
closer to me than God or my mother ever was.

Her walnut face powdered in the pink of another era,
my grandmother stooped and shrunk under the burden
of her Welsh past in the narrow valley and the weight of
all her lost ones; brothers buried under the fibrous collapse of
the pit, women screaming, running, shawls wrapped round
their heads, aprons flapping white as memorial doves:
they've gone, bach, they've gone, they've gone, don't cry, don't...
Those sweet boy's faces compressed into fossils under the
smothering earth black cracked with coal and no
getting them out; the service held above where they might be,
blessing all the earth just in case and my grandmother crying in the rain.

She was to marry a boy who played the piano, lovely hands he had,
his long face pale as a white petal, skin like old silk, coughing scarlet
coughing and coughing, dying, playing music like mountain torrents:
sometimes he came to her at night while she thought I slept saying
Lily, my lily of the valley, when will you come to me Lily girl, how I
                                              love you...
but he was a twist of vapour in the heavy hot night, gone in the rise
of her breathing, gone with her husband who burst his
congested heart clotted with terrible secrets, gone with her
golden son flying round the room in his rage, flying above the stars.

Oh, cut the cards, read the tea leaves, grandmother, look at my hand
will I live long, will I marry a handsome man – why are you gone away
behind your eyes leaving me alone with this inheritance of ghosts and the
bright unravelling skeins of the future messed and tangled

in the cloudy depths of what those who cannot see call the Sight;
turning under your still hand the hurts subsided, the pain released,
long bones eased; you could heal anyone, anyone – but not yourself.

Gone years ago now to join the wreath of your dead grandmother,
woven in amongst them tight as an early rose, now I see the spirits you
bequeathed me, my eyes fixed on things beside, beyond, and long,

long gone.

Home

We all carry a burden
walking through the years with this stone in our hearts,
so many miles with this stone, with this weight;
everyone has secrets, everyone wants to go home.

Home is more than fire and food,
more than a roof and a bed;
you can have it all – and still not be able to set that burden down;
everyone has secrets, everyone wants to go home.

Put it down for a moment as you stand in the dark;
put down the stone and stand up straight;
just for a moment, be free of the weight,
everyone has secrets, everyone wants to go home.

I'll be your home if you let me,
I'll carry your burden for a while if you want;
blood and bone, not hearth and stone,
everyone has secrets, everyone wants to go home.

Bradford

The wind blows hard today, across the city
lying crouched in its deep-sided valley.
The air is laced with the smell of clean stone
and the dusty purple heather that drapes
across the far horizon like a dropped scarf.
If I stop and listen I can almost hear,
faintly, like the faded thread of a song from an older age,
the cries of foxes that dance
in the moorland coverts and the blurred whirring
of kestrels riding the soaring thermals.

I walk over the crest of the hill and start down into Town,
past the intricate raggle of little shops that
embroider the road side and spill their
treasures onto the pavements.
All the world is here, laid out in patchworks
of drenched and brilliant colour;
dazzling pyramids of oranges from Morocco
like clotted sun, topiary broccoli, dark
green flounced cabbages and rich spinach,
feathery plumes of coriander and
gleaming scarlet apples bursting with temptation.
We want for nothing – watermelon, tender papaya,
smooth, languorous mangoes and luminous persimmons;
sometimes there are figs, their smart suede skins
the colour of bruises hiding gritty red flesh
so sweet, it tastes like the perfumed breath of angels.
I eat them with good Greek bread,
baked by serious Ukrainian men, craftsmen,
and I smile, thinking, in this town, we can eat like
princes for a pauper's fee.

I fill my bag with fruit and wander on,
window-shopping, my eye caught by the fabric shops
that burst with rolls and bolts of lace, and lamé
metallic and dangerous as deep water,
with satin, crepe and polyester
crusted with sequins, bullion and tiny mirrors,

foil stamped, hologrammed and photo-printed,
fabric patterned in every possible way;
striped and checked, hazy with impossible flowers,
stark with calligraphic motifs repeating and repeating
unknown phrases in an unknown tongue.

Brilliant as some dead caliph's treasure
the windows blaze with textile gems;
sapphire and emerald; ruby, heavy turquoise
and white that glimmers with the blue sheen of
Chomolungma's distant snows.
One window is all pinks; from summer's dusky rose
through bubblegum, shocking to a
shell pink so faint it's hardly breathing.
And best of all, so beautiful it makes me sigh,
a half unrolled length of pure, gleaming
silk that fades from blood red to the pink
of a desert sunset and back again.

But I walk on, down into the valley and the
secret stone puzzle that's the City.
Above me far overhead, wind-driven clouds unfurl
like great tattered banners, whipping through the blue
like flying prayers; they twist and roil like a time-lapse film,
cinematic, impossible and always with us in
this place so dominated by vast, untameable skies.

Stark against the huge backdrop of the clouds stand
the monumental sandstone buildings,
the Wool Barons' proud and unflinching legacy,
palaces of trade that couldn't be built now,
will never be built again by modern hands
no longer trained to patience and the skills
that turned the primeval bones of earth into carvings
as dense and intricate as nature herself.

Glancing up I see faces, plants and creatures made from stone
decorating every cornice, edge and buttress;
petrified sailing ships in full rig and portraits of
adamantine queens in medallions set on the
slab-sides of crumbling, forgotten towers.

Camels stride past pyramids cut out of stone by
men who would never see such things for themselves.
In the hundred niches that pock the great cliff of city hall
blind saints and craggy kings gaze into nothing
bound by masonry ropes and sandstone swags of ivy.
On other walls, griffins perch on acanthus twists
and arabesques, curlicues and cutwork
so deep you can stick your fingers in it
foam, twine and snake up spires that
reach greedily for the golden light that daily
turns their crushed crystals to living amber
for a few brief moments of glory...

I go to the Wool Exchange, that Temple to
the trade that made the city famous;
high up under the canopy of its arching,
ribbed roof that vaults to a ridge
like a mediæval galleon upturned,
and beached on a city street,
painted wooden archangels crowned in antique gold pray
with knotted, steepled hands.
Once they were mute witnesses to the swirl and play of money
on the trading floor beneath them,
now the city seraphim watch ordinary people
buying books and drinking coffee;
but they don't mind – they stretch their stiff, gilded wings
over everyone, young and old, and we're all in their charge.

And I sit down for a minute, amongst the books
and think of the town, stretching out and away
from here; dark and bright, beautiful and ugly,
the high-sided wind-scoured canyons of the deserted mills
telling their silent stories of what has been and what will be;
the deaths, the births, the fighting and the love,
all the humanity of it, gathered from every place in the world,
and all of us, everything, under the infinite night-sky now,
a silver twist of crescent moon fragile as a girl's first earring
visible even over the streetlights' sodium glare,
and I think – this is where we live, in this stone maze,
in this northern city, under the terrible stars, and we *belong*.

12

Friend

For Finn Mac Cool

You are sleeping on my bed;
I watch the narrow ribbed bellows
of your chest rising and falling
with your breath, with the heat
of your rapid, hunter's heart.

I see the dreaming twitch of paws,
their blades withdrawn into velvet,
the tattered, delicate arch of ears
and your muzzle, once shading
ochre to cream, now fading grey.

I stroke your leg, the fragile bones
articulating beneath the skin like
ancient jewellery and you open your eyes,
your great shining topaz eyes
and trusting, you close them again.

Because you know I will not harm you.

You know I would never harm you.

Dylan Thomas

When you talk about him; (you know *Dylan*, man;
Thomas, the Welsh one, the poet, not Bob, the other one)
when you talk about Dylan, using his ocean-boy,
fish-slippery name like you knew him, with that
oh-yeah-him drawl; when you talk about him,
being careful to add it's not your thing of course,
all that windy old poets' stuff, the spume of verbiage,
the sentimental dense baroquery of tears;
when you talk about him,
remember to mention

his writing.

Because the rest, the rest of it and the unrestful,
rat's nest mess of it, the drink-devilled, Hell's gate,
puking in fireplaces and pissing the bed,
the threadbare fumey fat-fingered fondling,
the begging, finagling and false promises;
the beer-barrel brawling; the death-by-proxy
spectacle that drew the eager arse-kissing crowds at toney
up-town parties and left a maggotty banquet of misbegotten
half-truths and the gnawed carcasses of stories for the
scavengers, feverishly buffing up the glittery fragments
of their ripped-off two-minute fame,
to pick through daintily; all those yarns about
the wife – brute, ruined girl – the camp-followers,
the fifteen straight whiskies and the indestructible velvet voice

that stuff is a distraction.

It makes you forget the brilliant boy, possessed by, mad for, words,
those roaring and whispering anthracite worm-casts of the Celtic
soul all tumbling cross-wise and cat's cradle from his trembling
white hands – moist with passion, tattooed with ink – as he scrivened
like a sin-eater feasting on death-sweet forbidden words, words, words
under the bright, baying moon.

Oh God oh God let me never lose this gift let me never be a dry and
rattling husk of myself empty empty and it all gone away

But the gift was cursed. It always is. And the curse was writ
big and dandy-dark through our Dylan's widdershins and warped DNA;
It's the oldest curse of all that says (chanted in the powdery black ash night
by wild Welsh witches in tall hats and chorused by neglected children);
you don't get anything for nothing: And he didn't.

We don't.

And the more you get given, brother, the more you pay;
so don't forget, as you suck the
gossip off your greasy
fingers, to mention
his writing.

Fortune Favours the Tattooed Heart

'Fortune Favours The Tattooed Heart' was a motto
pinned up in old fashioned tattoo studios
where bent-backed men crouched over their sparking machines
and tattooed sailors with galleons called 'Homeward'.
High-masted, top-heavy, full-rigged with myriad sails
and running forever in front of impossible gales;
those indigo ships brought you luck on the sea,
brought you home safe from the terrible mystery of the World.

Or maybe a velvety rose, redder than real blood ever was,
bloomed on the blank canvas of a boy's arm,
its thorny viridian stems bound with banners reading
'True Love' or a girl's name – 'Stella', 'Amy' or 'Rita';
names that faded into ghostly blue as skin withered and
life trickled its slow unstoppable hourglass sand away,
leaving, in soft calligraphy, the sweet half-forgotten
memory of youth and first passion's bright hectic dazzle.

There's a language of tattoo pictures, a true narrative made of
four-petalled flowers, broken crimson hearts, daggers plunging
through deathless phrases about honour and pride.
It speaks about distant dreams of cherry-blossom Geisha girls
twirling their paper parasols, it chants the gambler's prayers
made flesh in lucky eight-balls and the Ace Of Spades,
the pin-up angel of Chance reclining in her champagne glass;
this is our heritage – these are our icons, our ancestor memories.

And every generation brings their own pictures,
their desires, their omens and their loves to the oldest art
humanity has practised – a river of ink flows from our
First Mother, gazing at the ochre dust of a distant desert,
marking her forehead or her arm with a flint and soot
through to the everlasting braid of Celtic interlock and the emerald
brocade dragon clinging to a shoulder; voices clamouring in the
golden lotus,the Japanese carp, bright impossible butterflies, and lost
gods.

Through the great turning dance of life the skill came with us;
in every culture, in every land we tattooed ourselves.
Scythian princesses, Christian pilgrims, Roman soldiers, Bedouin riders,
Pacific islanders, grand duchesses and English kings,
dancers and thieves, scholars and jewelled courtesans;
some offered their blood and pain to faith and some for beauty,
some shouted their allegiance or saluted their country;
but nothing stopped us creating this art, and nothing will ever stop us.

We do it because we can mark ourselves out amongst the
teeming millions of our species that break in an unending tide
on the beautiful Earth; we can own something that cannot be taken
from us, we can say with the bright mythology of our skins,
I am Myself: the tokens *I* chose now live in me; look at them
and you look at *me*, see them and you see the map of my spirit,
and whatever fate sends me, I will have the consolation of my
tattooed heart until my last breath comes and
I close my eyes forever in that long sleep.

Talisman

Commissioned by The Captain Cook Museum, Whitby

The girdling ocean circles the earth layered in sheer
translucent blue, sequinned with the salt-silver
sparkle of fish and shot through from Pole to Pole
with the bone-deep harmonics of whale-song;
its surface – that bright shifting, shimmering veil,
is kissed by the skimming pinions of sea birds
dancing from island to island through the vast and
tender sapphire air or the dark masses of coiling storms,
while at its sweeping hem, the breakers pale lace ruffles
on grey stone quays and crushed shell strands alike.

Over and over, brine touches sand, sand touches turf
and high cliffs tumble down embroidered with
sharp shivering sprays of marram, the jaunty thrust
of sea pinks or the tattered opulence of hibiscus:
Cup the dissolving fretwork of sea-foam in your hands and
know it came to this cold, wind-harried Northern place
from the great dreaming beauty of the Pacific:
We all drift on the ocean, we are all Her children,
our bodies mostly water, our hearts surging with the tides.

All those who move upon the sea are brothers and sisters;
bound in the great romance of navigation by the stars,
gull-path and dolphin-road, the white horses' mad gallop.
Blood runs salt and eyes are bleached by the long gaze
at far horizons tilting with the deck's roll and yaw
or the hard judder of the oars' sinew-cracking dip and haul:
And all mariners have their ciphers, on charts or on the skin;
all sailors crave the comfort of luck in the face of the cool infinity,
in the sight of the vast unknowable and melancholy waters.

Mother Thalassa marks her own; the tattoo ageing blue
as the far depths is one way; a prayer to Her for protection:
Jack Tar had his indigo galleons or his grinning skull and cross-bones;
the Polynesians took as their safe-travelling totem the
long-tailed Frigate Bird, who catches fish at sea but eats on land,

a beloved fluttering guide to follow gratefully to safe haven;
they tapped the stylised icon of the little fisher-bird into their flesh
with a sharp staccato beat, counterpointed by the old magic chants
that fixed the spirit and the holy grace into the image forever.

Sailors from the North who bore the ceremony and the pain
to catch a little of the Southern luck, took the Frigate Bird home
on hand or breast; exotic, foreign in the bustling ports of England
and saw, over the years, it become a bright western Swallow,
mutating through long usage and half-understood myths
into the sweet, familiar symbol of golden summers in
country lanes or sleepy villages and the true origin of the
long-tailed lucky piece was forgotten – but it continued
spinning its curious quiet spell through generation after generation.

The oceans pull with the moon; mariners flow out from harbours
in outriggers, schooners, tall ships, barques, kayaks, whalers and junks,
and the Swallow returned, in time, to its strange ancestor's homelands;
there it was tattooed with the electric machine's sharp piercing hum
on Polynesians wanting a taste of the Western dream, the new style,
the chance of some far distant, other world good fortune;
and the circle starts to close upon itself just as the sea serpent
eats his tail in the dark abyssal cold of the deep-sea trench;
the old enchantment working its pattern out across the globe.

I have Frigate Birds, flying in their stiff archaic way on my hands now;
a Maori put them there, two of them done in the old way,
bone needle dipped in black, prayers said before the work commenced.
They are my talismans, they see me safe around the world and back again.
I have great faith in their ancient and unwavering certainty,
they complete the vision and the oldest family of all;
a tribe of travellers wandering the compass and the night sea
caught in the unconscious passion of the nomadic soul,
all of us neither of the land or of the sea, but deep in love with both.

Holy Medal

We bought them on our honeymoon in Spain;
I love Spanish things, don't you?
And being Catholic, I – we – thought it was
such a lovely idea...

A pair of holy medals of the Blessed Virgin;
identical, but his was in gold,
that good, eighteen carat foreign gold
and mine was silver...

I could have had the gold, he wanted me to;
but in those days I thought silver was nicer,
I thought it looked more elegant and in my opinion,
gold was for the older woman...

We never took them off, those pendants, never;
I can see them in the photos,
I can see him in the photos, smiling.
He was always smiling...

Then he died – it was very sudden;
the doctors were marvellous but it was no good
and I buried him with his medal,
just as he would have wanted...

But then, I couldn't rest, I couldn't rest
for wishing that I'd got the gold pendant
not the silver; I wanted us to be the same, you see,
I wanted us to be connected...

So I had mine gold-plated and for a while
it looked lovely, just like his, and I took great care
of it, not going swimming in it or anything;
when I wore it, I felt he was with me again...

But the plating came off, they said it wouldn't
but it did – and the medal looked awful, peeling, decayed;

I couldn't wear it, I couldn't think of him that way,
and now, he's gone forever...

We bought them on our honeymoon in Spain,
they make lovely things, the Spanish;
two medals of the Blessed Virgin, for luck, for protection,
oh, Holy Mother, Holy Mother – why didn't I have the gold...

The Rose

One year, when we were in Spain for Christmas,
walking in the icy sun and frosted shadows,
the dun and ochre, lavender and mulberry
hills stepping away from the white town
in layer after layer of ancient memories,
we bought a rose; a bare-root shrivelled
stick of a thing, cased in harsh green wax
against pests and disease,
a tiny withered leaf, fluttering at the tip
of one small, fragile branch.

Back home, in my city yard,
I planted it in a great, blue-painted pot,
and waited for nothing, like gardeners do;
not hoping, never wishing, containing disappointment
and expecting only that it would die.

This year, the Spanish rose bloomed
in a mass of huge dark red flowers, so crimson,
so arterially scarlet and so thirsty for life
the flounced petals seem lit from within
by a blaze; seem incandescent, like rubies
held against the sun – the pigeon's blood rubies
of old legends, intense colour springing from
the final outpouring of the poor, captive bird's life blood.

The rose bloomed in summer and again, this September;
more flowers than ever, brighter than you'd think possible
in the second growth, glowing against grey Autumn skies,
more bloody, more vivid and more precious.

But September winds here in the North
are cold and killing; sweeping in from far places
and carrying, this year, a fine black dust; in the keening storm
a fine, black dust that smothered the velvet petals
of those red roses, that scattered them in the dirt and blown rubbish.

September winds are cold and killing,
sometimes it seems that spring will never come again...

Sometimes it seems that spring will never come again.

The Archangel Michael

I am in love with the Archangel Michael; the Goddess' warrior prince,
the soldier of glory; at my back he stands lambent, violent, pure;
the punishing sweep of his great wings lock forward around me
as I struggle in the darkness seeking what he already
knows is truth and what I must find my own way to through pain and ruin.

My Archangel; not a man but a creature made of night and amber fire,
his golden eyes fixed on distances beyond my understanding or my little life
and he moves in the high places of the perilous World, his mouth a curved
unsmiling bow from which no arrow dare be loosed and his armour
gleams shadow-bronze chased in arabesques of purity.

Beautiful, beautiful Michael, as cruel as youth and as gentle as a brother's
kiss he comforts me as I weep and when my heart boils with blood:
His arm around my waist he holds me steady and we breathe together,
the angel and I, until the soft cool of dawn turns the hills to mist and
memory.
He dwells in all lands, wherever I run to he follows and I see him in
the sea-foam or the mountain's cruel escarpment.

He was in Africa, my Michael, when I tried to fight and lost, I brought him
home with me in a Congo fetish, the Spear-Thrower.
N'kissi N'kondi he is called in the dust and terror, the nail studded
punisher of wrongdoers, reeking of wood-fires and spice, his old brown face
wick and radiant, more alive than the living,
filled with power and the hot push of fury.
I leave him water in a little black bowl sometimes, but he doesn't care.

All he cares about is justice, all Michael cares about is justice and knowing that,
oh, knowing that, I am in love with the Archangel Michael,
I am in love with faith and beauty.

Always faith and beauty.

The Prophet Of Calgary

I came here from the north of England
many years ago now; I came with Jim
away from the smoke and the crouching
huddles of buildings black as coal.

All I had there was a typist's job,
a chilly, damp room in a boarding house,
the notebooks full of poetry I'd tried to write and
no family to speak of; I took no persuading to leave.

We had a good life here, in the big, bright city
ringed with rearing mountains,
the hard blue dome of the sky above and air and space
like we'd never dreamed of back at home.

Now I come every day to sit on this bench,
always the same bench, in the square by the
big shopping mall, deep in the icy canyons
of high buildings that leap upwards like glittering crystal spires.

The air here is like a steel razor; it slices as it pours
into your lungs, you can feel blood in your breath;
I get quite dizzy and when I do the angels come,
dancing round me in shimmering sprays of frost.

What a glory they are; etched like twists of
crushed glass in the white fire of the winter day,
and how they whisper to me, their voices the
high and wire-thin tone of ice-floes breaking:

Anne, Anne you are a prophet; we are the
love of God, see our beauty, see the glory
of heaven in our frozen eyes, hear us sing like
mountain winds, we are the angels of the Lord...

And they float around me, massed in prisms of unearthly light,
sheaves of angels, stark and bleached as the snow-killed,

wings beating, beating in hollow silence while the molten
ball of the setting sun burns glacial in the great windows.

Sometimes young people come and bring me food;
they talk about me as if I can't hear them,
they're kind and they mean well, but they look at me
and only see what the poor, lost, world sees.

They try to take me to the hospital where it's warm;
look at her fingers, they say, *look at her cheeks,
it's frost bite, why won't she come with us?*
But it's not frost bite and I cannot leave

I have been kissed by angels...

Venice

The old boat clatters through the Grand Canal;
it's near midnight and cold; the water we plough
through is like ink, the rotting, ruined palaces
haunted by money and dead countesses
are whiter than paper; crumpled, spoiled paper
folded into these sinking facades.

The great dome of the Salute is a dead pearl
festooned with charnel statues paler than bones,
dirty and sightless, a slipped wreath
of twisted saints and straining prelates
reaching towards heaven from their precarious
perches, feet frozen, slipping, stone mouths yawing.

When day comes in a vapour of mist
we walk the tight-bound, teetering streets
with no room to pass, no space to turn in,
no milky flawed opal sky visible,
just round and round, past the cafes empty
of summer tourists and vain churches empty of voices.

On one old wall, the Holy Mother spreads
her carved cloak wide to protect the tiny people
clustered at her feet; Magna Mater, her face eaten
by age and pollution, blunt and blind;
would She give me, if I asked Her,
a blue Venetian glass heart, like the ones they

sell in every shop we pass; a small thing,
like a child's jewel, a dressing-up necklace
that you could lose in the salt crash of the sea
and not regret, that would catch the sun like a drop of sky...
Would She give me, do you think, a blue glass heart
to replace my broken one?

Tatiana

In the rosy bruise of the Slavic dusk
Tatiana stands in the orchard, waiting.

Around her the old apple trees, white
with blossom, dance like foolish brides
in the dusty wind and Tatiana blinks
her wolf's eyes, clear grey as meltwater,
and waits, the holy medal glinting at her throat.

It is turning colder as the snow veiled mountains
exhale their icy night breath and Tatiana's old
cotton dress is thin with wear; she shivers, once,
all over her thin body and clenches her fists
against the failing light. She is tired of waiting.

Her face is illuminated, ivory, heiratic;
her thick curling hair, the colour of old bronze,
pulled back tightly; her mouth, compressed
as a frost-nipped rosebud, keeps her secrets
and her fierce desire contained.

Tatiana is not waiting for a lover, she has none:
An old woman, walnut brown and bent as a willow
told her if she said certain things, at a certain time,
and stood where life bursts yet again from the ancient trees
the ghost of her mother would return and comfort her.

So Tatiana waits, tears seeding those feral eyes,
for the warm touch of love long lost while
a storm of petals slowly hides her from sight;
and for one brief second, one savage leaping heartbeat,
she feels she is not alone.

Tatiana walks home along the ochre road
and weeps, but does not make a sound.

The Wolf Girls Of Midnapore

They shot the mother wolf straight away,
the short dark arrows taking her in the throat
and chest as she stood, snarling, braced
against the entrance to the den where her cubs lay hidden.
To give him his due, the Reverend Singh tried to prevent
the villagers from killing her but this was 1920
and in the jungles of India wolves were vermin;
as far as the men were concerned,
it was one less pest to worry about.

Then the villagers caught the cubs,
which were valuable and could be sold at the market
for a good price, and were about to shoot the two ghosts
that growled and spat amongst the blood and dust,
but Singh stopped them – not without some difficulty
since the men could not understand why he was
so keen to save a pair of forest demons,
the same devils they had begged him to come and exorcise.

But Singh had seen at once that the ghosts
were human children – though their years with the
wolves had altered their bodies beyond redemption.
They had adapted to their wild life, become strange,
their filthy little faces hardly visible under matted
balls of hair that trailed to the floor.
He noted in his journal how the girl's jaws had
become muscular, powerful from cracking bones
and tearing flesh; their teeth yellow and elongated,
especially the eye teeth, the canines.
Their spines had stretched and become more flexible, too,
just as their elbow and knee joints had grown knotted
and thickly callused from running on all fours.
Most unnerving of all, Singh wrote, were
their enlarged eyes that gleamed with
white disks of phosphorescence in the gathering dusk
and flickered with unnatural rapidity, like a beast's.

Singh took the girls to his orphanage and the care
of his wife who shaved their heads and
washed them clean as they writhed and scratched,
fighting the stink of soap and shivering from the water.
They were baptised and called Amala and Kamala,
auspicious names that they never answered to
as they padded round and round the compound at night
in the heavy, jasmine scented air; the great swollen moon
the only light they wanted as they called to their
pack brothers so far away to come and save them from this horror.

But no-one came; no strong sinewy shadow leapt the
stockade to carry them home and so they became pets of a sort.
The Singhs tried to train them to be human again
so they could be good Christian girls and
return to society, perhaps even marry one day
and forget their feral childhood, forget their singing blood.
But it was hopeless: The girls slept in a tangled huddle,
inseparable as puppies, eating only raw meat,
never learning to stand upright comfortably,
never making friends or understanding why they should,
attacking the other children if they teased them,
their blunt, unsmiling faces blank, their only reference point each
other.

Then, after a year, Amala died, scoured by fever and dysentery,
her belly bloated with parasitic worms,
her distorted body racked with stinking sweats,
the pain making her bite at anyone who came near her,
except Kamala, who licked her clean and
curled around her through the heat of the day,
mewling and grunting frantically as her sister drifted away from her.

At the point of Amala's dying, Kamala threw her head back
and howled, her long, corded neck working convulsively
and she shed tears, the only time in her life she did so,
then she fell on her sister's cooling body
and would not be comforted or distracted from her grief.

She did not live much longer; although the Singhs had tried
to prevent it, the Wolf Girls Of Midnapore had become celebrities,
journalists tricked their way in to the orphanage
and wrote thrilling pieces about the Savage Children
who ran naked like animals and had no shame.
The world soon goggled at pictures of Kamala kneeling
in her un-human way at Mrs. Singh's feet and feeding
from her hand, docile, tamed by her terrible loneliness.

She was to be exhibited in America, a tour
was planned, shows booked, tickets sold...
But she died the same way her sister had;
finally escaping her captivity.

She never learned to say her name.

In one photograph, taken before Amala died,
the girls have been put into ill-fitting white dresses
and are crouched, staring just past the camera lens at
whoever is taking the picture.
There is no comprehension in their eyes,
no sense of knowing what is happening,
no interest in it.

They look like dogs dressed in doll's clothes.

Not so very different then, from the rest of us.

Hrothgar's Queen

My hair is like sun-gold white wind blown wheat;
it falls in rippled lengths to my knees when my
women unbraid it, and I say I have never cut it, but I lie.
My eyes are pieces of summer sky cut out
and rounded under the glossy shell-curve
of my eyelids and I say I have never wept, but I lie.

I am beautiful; understand, this is not immodesty
but the currency my world balances on,
my father's fortunes invested in my lily skin
and strong, high-breasted, round-hipped height.
One year I was the corn-maid;
I was of course, being my father's daughter, the popular choice.
I was dressed in all the tender sap-sprung shades of green,
girdled with a twist of ivy and crowned
with white flowers, their pale petals falling
as the day grew hot and the spring dancing
whirled me dizzy, man after man grasping my
hands and flinging me through the ancient steps
that could not, for me, a princess, end in the
night of love the other girls boasted of and
displayed in their god-blessed swelling bellies.
I envied them that; they envied my jewels
and my ribbons – baubles I'd let go as easily as a tree
sheds dead leaves in Autumn I valued them so little.

I often say, with a graceful sigh and dreamy gaze,
that I have loved only my husband, the king,
and all the gods know *that* is a lie.
I did love once, like a girl should; fever bright
and heady, praying with a sudden devotion
that we should meet, my beloved and I,
by chance in the stable or the
far, sheltering and tangled wild of the demesne.
He was my father's man, a fosterling
with the pure, dedicated face of a fighting boy,
hardly a scar on him, and a mouth that I would

drink from as a bee does from a ripe, sun-hot blossom...
Because I was young, I thought our love was secret;
I discovered my mistake all too soon.

My father beat me, his hand wrapped in the thick tresses of my hair
to control me, as he did with the mane of an unbroken mare.
I screamed and twisted, my body bucking and thrashing
away from his blows and the fate I knew awaited me.
My mother mewled and moaned beside us, pleading for
him not to mark my face, the coin that would buy them
an alliance with Hrothgar; that would keep our lands safe.
I called my beloved's name and my father laughed;
harsh and without pity, then had my mother's woman
examine me to be sure I was still of use.

She was an old, old woman; older than the raven-black
night that closed its suffocating wings around us as she handled me.
Her face was a drought-cracked landscape of hard living
and I could not believe she had ever been young or straight-backed.
The other women whispered that she served two queens;
my mother, and that dark, ancient Lady who never dies,
the Old Mother who dwells in the hidden groves
and magic, painted caves and who we, as civilised folk,
scorn to worship and pretend we do not know.
I hated that old hag, hated her mottled hands that
touched me as if I were an animal to be gentled,
hated her age and the evidence of my own future, I hated her...
Then she put her withered mouth to my ear and told
me with a wheezy chuckle the truth I didn't want to hear;
'as I am, so will you be, my lady'.
Then she said my beloved had been whipped at the post
but that he lived, and was being taken to his own people
to be nursed – then he was to return because his family
was strong and my father had no wish to offend them
over a silly girl's folly; I said I didn't care.
How many lies I have told.

My marriage to Hrothgar was great in state and circumstance,
I had many new gowns and my lord's wedding gift
was a double rope of amber beads the size of

sea-washed pebbles, that came down to my knees
in gleaming drops of golden honey.
I was washed in spring-water and camomile and my yellow
hair braided in a coil to hide the short lengths I'd hacked off
in my fury and that had not yet grown long.

Hrothgar put the queen's crown, red-gold and leaping
like a circlet of fire, on my head himself.
I promised to serve him and the land, and to grace his hearth,
I promised, and under my long sleeves with
my eyes cast down in maidenly modesty,
I crossed my fingers like a child as I spoke the lies.

I was fifteen years old.

Hrothgar was past forty, grizzled and slack skinned;
his teeth were rotten in his head and his breath stank like a midden.

I was still just a girl, and I burned for my beloved
even as Hrothgar mounted me like the old ram he was
panting and juddering; afterwards, my virgin's bloody sheets
hanging from the window, he patted my fevered head
and gave me a heavy gold and amber ring to match my beads.
It turned loose on my finger and later the women said it
was his first wife's, who had died in childbirth.
When he left, I washed myself out with vinegar;
I wanted no child of his, I wanted no part of him in me,
no flesh of his in mine, and I cried so hard
the women begged me to stop in case I spoiled my eyes,
my sky blue, sea blue, cornflower blue eyes.

Half a year later, as I grew skinny and my complexion
waned like the dying moon they sent my mother's woman to me;
the Mother's woman, gnarled and grimy as an old pine tree.
She cackled when she saw me and said she had a cure for all my ills.
In my fury, I ordered her away, but she would not leave.
I threw my pretty bronze mirror at her but
she ducked and laughed again, her seamed face lit with mischief.
Then she told me of my beloved's new wife,
plump and comely, already swelling with his child and both

of them happy as nesting doves.
Then she held me while I wept for the last time and cursed the gods,
and when my lord came that night she sent him away,
saying I was unwell, a woman's sickness, and he went quickly
like men do at such times.

That night, she told me what it was to be a queen;
she told me about power and the getting of it,
about the management of men and royal houses
and all that could be mine *if* I had the stomach for it.
I heard the truth in her croak of a voice
and it filled me with a passion that made me cry out.
I vowed that all she spoke of I would have, and more.
I would never again be helpless or under anyone's dominion.
So I went with her, out into the velvet midnight forest,
to the secret, high and solitary place she knew,
I made the sacrifice, spoke the words and had the mark put on me;
here, see? On my ankle, very faint, like smoke,
like the bitter smoke of the herb strewn fire
she lit that night that brought the Mystery and my fate.

The next day I smiled and looked under my eyelashes
at my lord and told him I was well, I was very well,
that I would be pleased to receive him that night
and I touched his wrist with soft, scented fingers
and felt the pulse in it jump a little, just a little, at my command.
So it was I became a queen and took the reins
in my white hands, and ruled as women always have,
each night growing a little stronger, with every whispered
confidence a little bolder, until *nothing* my lord did,
did not go through me; no mercenary paid, no princeling bought,
no lands seized, no rebellion subdued, no strategy planned,
but that it all grew from the seeds planted in those nightly visits.
And always, *always*, he believed he thought of it all himself
and I praised his cleverness, his potency
until my tongue grew heavy in my mouth and he
snored and twitched in his sleep like an old dog chasing dream rabbits.

And that spring, my lord built Heorot, that
most extravagant, most beautiful of buildings
for me as a gift; because he thought I loved him truly.

Lies built Heorot; it was a monument to lies
and the dream of love; Heorot, home of heroes,
the bright-painted, oak raftered proof of my power.

It was my mother's woman first told me of
the Old Blood boy she had seen skulking
round the walls at night; she walked in the still dark
for her herbs and for other things I did not enquire of.
He watches, she said, *he is a prince among the*
Old Ones, my queen; he prays to the Moon Mother
to destroy you, beware of him when he grows to his strength.
She said she had dealings with his dam,
one of their wise women, a priestess and their queen;
there was some secret about the boy though she did not understand,
the old speech being difficult and strange.
I told my lord that night; warned him that
I had heard the Old Ones were a danger to be reckoned with
not merely the brute savages we thought them.
But for once, he scoffed and dismissed my words,
then reached for his ale, saying he would take the time
one of these days to rid the land
of that creeping vermin; perhaps a hunting party,
that would amuse the thanes; he'd make a contest of it
with rewards for kills, a jewel-set gold torc for the most
heads hung by their long black braids,
bouncing at the winner's saddle bow.

So it was that summer the killing started in earnest;
I was annoyed my lord went against my advice,
I thought it ill-judged to create an enemy where none
had been before – but my lord and his thanes wanted
sport as there was no war in the offing for them to enjoy.
As the days passed, the heads of the slaughtered
lay heaped in high, crazy piles in the midden yard,
steaming and skin-ripped, black-studded with flies;
my maidens puked and ran, fluttering like tearful little butterflies
while the men laughed hot and hard at their distress.
My mother's woman pulled her shawl over her head and
muttered charms against ill-luck while every night Heorot

rang with the drunken shouts of men who did not
bother to clean the Old Ones' blood from their hands before they ate.
But soon their sport was over; the game ran out,
and they hung the hall with polished skulls for trophies and
Unferth, my lord's favourite, got the gold torc
though it was said he bought his heads from the huntsmen,
coward that he is – I congratulated him and turning my back
for a moment, spat in the ale I gave him so graciously...
A woman's trick, but satisfying.

Years went past; I forgot that summer, the Old Ones,
the boy that had hidden in the shadows, watching.
That was my curse, that forgetting, that was my error,
the price the gods exacted for giving me power.
I knew I had forgotten something, it galled like a sore,
twitching at the edges of my mind as I organised banquets
and received visitors, and tended my duties
with the smile that never touched my sky-bright eyes,
the eyes that love-sick bards called Odin's most precious jewels,
or sea-sapphires sparkling, set in an ivory spear.
Fools, poets, all of them; all bought by a coin
and a place at the feasting – a woman who believes
their cant deserves her fate for being as
fond and foolish as those wandering scoundrels herself.

Time flowed past steady and inexorable, a river heavy with silt,
rich and fertile and I grew stronger every hour.
But time took my mother's woman, too;
she died in my arms, light as a dry bone,
made brittle as a sea-shell by the crab that
ate her vitals; her crow-voice torn raw from screaming.
I gave her the drink that eased her from the world myself.
It was the least I could do, and I puzzled
at her last croaking words;
'beware, my queen, the boy is grown'.
The boy? What boy? I had no boy, no son, no child;
no flesh of Hrothgar's line distracted me
from my work and my lord's besotted adoration;
no puking brat thickened my waist or leeched the
bloom from my cheeks and Hrothgar had long since

named his eldest fosterling his heir;
a lumpen, ruddy faced fool who blushed
and trembled like a girl when I laid
a cool hand on his already-balding pate.
He would be no trouble to me, so who was the boy?

My mother's woman was scarce buried
before I found out, found what my forgetting had cost.
The boy was Grendel, and he rose from the deep
and distant moorlands, from the ragged, hidden fastnesses
owl-haunted, lost and damned that were his people's
last refuges; now he was the Lord of the Marches,
prince of the dark tarns, and true son of the
Old Ones' Priestess, the dark and secret queen,
my mirror image and my nemesis; Grendel rose in his might
and his people's archaic glory and he came to Heorot
to destroy the enemy – to destroy us – to destroy my world.

Grendel, the last war-lord of the Old Ones;
the avenger of his people and the greatest murderer
the world has ever known.

Black-haired, he came, out of the haunted night,
his braided serpent locks threaded with flowers
like a bridegroom, with death his bride to be;
his body painted with warrior's charms so strong,
so thick with ancient sorcery that spears turned
and blades broke before they even grazed him.
He blazed amongst our fat drink sodden thanes
slashing throats and smashing skulls to sodden pulp;
he howled like an animal, like a dire-wolf, as he stuffed
the still-beating hearts he tore from the blood-eagled
bodies of our warriors into his mouth, his white teeth
tearing at that forbidden meat, his peat-brown eyes
huge and burning with magic and hate and a fury so terrible,
so consuming and so world-rending
that no fear touched him and no man of ours
could stand against the hideous might of his killing rage.

Grendel, Grendel, Grendel – oh, the horror of him,
the brute unspeakable violence of him,
night after night; the blood sprayed like thrown water
on the bright paint of Heorot and I screamed until
my voice sounded like that old dying woman's as
she tried to warn me of the future; of this terror.

Then, one night as Heorot rang again with
the futile clash of weapons and men's death cries,
I could stand it no more and I ran out from my hiding place
with the women; as if compelled, I ran into the hall
and half-fainting with horror, hand to my mouth, I faced him,
saw the monster hacking and tearing flesh and bone
into bloody white-splintered collops with his
razor-lean leaf-shaped blade and his bare hands.
And he looked up from his labour and saw me,
he looked into my eyes and his clotted, dripping mouth
curved in a smile; *and I knew he knew me,*
knew who and what I was; knew I was Hrothgar's queen
and he laughed; then raising his sword, he saluted me.
The dark queen's unspeakable get saluted me,
insolent and proud, his tattooed face full of
intelligence and cruelty; his painted body wick and
burnished like a bronze shield; like my lord's had never been,
like my lord had never, ever been in all his life,
in all his youth long gone, in all the times I let him grunt
and plough me in my bed...
Grendel looked at me with those terrible, beautiful eyes
and my wyrd was upon me in a swift and deadly moment,
and I wanted him; he was my equal, he was as full of power,
as full of rage as I was and I wanted him
as a woman wants a man, truly wants a man,
greedy and insatiable; my body shook from wanting him
as I had wanted no man ever in my life.

I wanted Grendel, his fierce, glorious, appalling strength
that burned in him like wildfire set to turn the living world
to ash and cinders, and looking in my face he knew it
and he laughed again; he laughed, he laughed at my desire,
and I saw that I was nothing to him...

That's when I knew he had to die,
he and all his kin, no matter what the cost.

That night, that very night, as my lord sweated
and prayed yet again to a dozen different gods
I clenched my jaw, stilled my breathing and
spoke softly about the great hero Lord Beowulf,
whom the bards extolled and my women sighed over.
I talked of his magnificent bravery, his stainless reputation,
how he would be the very one to rid us of this demon,
this savage, feral brute, this unwarranted curse...
Beowulf would come if we pleaded for his help,
appealed to his strength, asked his protection,
let him know that others said Grendel was too
great an opponent for him, that it was believed by some
that no living man could slay a creature as hideous,
as monstrous and as devil-sent as Grendel the Tarn Lord.

That, I knew, would fetch a man like Beowulf
and we would get him cheap because of it.

My lord was very pleased with his idea to entice
the legendary hero to do his fighting for him;
another great victory for mighty Beowulf
and peace at last for poor, riven Heorot...

I had scarce set the rumours in motion when Beowulf
was with us, clattering up from the beach with his men,
leaving his swift war-boat to sleep grey and sleek
on the shining salt-glazed shingle.

In my most becoming gown, hair sun-bright and burnished,
my amber twined around my white throat and
with properly downcast eyes, I knelt and gave him the welcome cup,
murmuring how honoured, how privileged we were to
receive such a noble and brilliant warrior.
He barely glanced at me as he spoke the courtesies,
his iron link mail clinking soft and smooth with use,
his brown face like a stone-carved battle-god.

I raised my eyes to him but he did not see the sky in them
nor the corn silk of my hair, and I knew what manner
of man he was then; I had seen it before in other men
whose gaze fixed on far horizons and who heard only
the voice of their totems in the churning of their blood.
I sensed the berserker in him like you smell a storm coming;
a tang of metal and the dry hiss of lightening soon to strike.
It was all to obvious to me why he was such a hero;
he loved blood-letting like I loved to rule; it was his religion,
his faith, and he walked calm and sanctified with his gods.
I think in some hidden, incomprehensible way he was quite insane;
his perfect good manners a mask he held up as protection,
his cool, distant charm that set my maidens fluttering
a convenient disguise; only his men mattered to him,
his fellow devotees – it was all in those obsidian eyes
and in the fingers drumming on the chair-arm,
thrumming with some tense internal rhythm
his pulse ran to and his mind ran away from.

Not that night, nor the next, nor the next
did Grendel come; I prayed and cut a black cockerel's
throat with a flint edge each midnight as the spell dictated,
chanting until my brain swam and the acrid stink of burning
blood sizzling on the embers turned my guts,
but still he didn't come...

I dreamed of him; I felt his blood-wet mouth on mine
and my heart was gravid and sore in my fevered breast...

Then out of the dark and deadly distance; from beyond
the places our people dared to walk by night or day,
Grendel stepped like a king; like a sacrifice, willing and unbound.
For once, the doors of Heorot, newly oiled and silent,
swung open at his touch and on the threshold he paused,
his bright head cocked, puzzled by the unnatural quiet.
Then as he stood there, wondering, Beowulf rose like
an icy wave from his waiting-place by the skull-pile,
white firelight flickering down the wicked length
of his iron sword and he smiled his deadly welcome.

It was like a dance, that battle; I was minded of the steps
I trod round the corn-maid's fire so long ago;
intricate and full of intent, full of passion unspent.
They were perfectly matched; Beowulf and Grendel,
one ice, the other fire; containment and chaos.
Round and round they circled each other
silently, trapped in their strange marriage.
Around them no-one dared to move or breathe
or mutter prayers, no-one save myself and I prayed
hard and long in my heart for the death of my enemy, my love;
I prayed until my body ached and on the palms
of my hands, bloody nail-marks wept
where my fists had clenched in my agony.

Then they fought; I am no warrior, I cannot
say if they fought well, or badly, but I do know
I have never before seen men fight as if they were in
some ancient rite, as if each blow given and received
was long rehearsed, as if each knew exactly what
the other would do, where he would strike and how.

Then as we all stared transfixed, they locked blades,
the iron and the bronze, their faces almost touching
and over Beowulf's shoulder I saw Grendel's face
and in it, I saw death and the knowledge of his fate,
I saw the bursting heart of the past, in this, the final battle.

Then Grendel stepped back, and inclining his head
to Beowulf in some strange courtesy, extended his sword
as if to invite him to continue the dance;
but Beowulf swung his blade, the blood-drinker,
the widow-maker, the star-metal soul-taker,
swung it so hard I heard the sinews crack in his shoulders
and he severed Grendel's arm clean above the elbow.

Then I know I heard my women's screams blister
through the thick, white air that froze around me,
but nothing more, as I slid into a dark I hoped was death.

My lord had me taken, I'm told, to my chamber
and laid still and pale as cold wood ash on my great bed.
They thought my tender heart – *my tender heart* – had
stopped in terror at that ghastly sight and I was dead of it;
but I was not, however much I wished it to be so; I could not die.

But Grendel, yes, he died; and the dark queen, his mother
who they say fought like a fiend with the man who
killed her son; my lord was very pleased she died,
he seemed happier with that than with all the rest.
I wonder, had he known her, spoken with her?
She was very beautiful; by her head I knew this,
it was set on a long pike, with her child's, at our gates,
decaying like all mortal flesh and the stinking token of
my lord's – and Beowulf's, of course – magnificent victory.
The crows would not eat those dead eyes though, as they
usually do; strange that, my mother's woman would
have known the meaning of it, would have told me
what my lord was hiding behind that smug and smiling face.

Oh, I don't care, I don't care, I don't care;
I care for very little these days – it has been a long winter
and still the ice lies unbroken on the far tarns.
Yesterday, in the brief flicker of daylight I looked
at my long braid and saw grey in the gold of my hair...
I knew, too, that I shall have to send my new girl away,
who is as watchful and sinuous as a bitch otter and who
my lord asked last night to pour his ale.

Time takes us all, in the end; Grendel, Beowulf,
Hrothgar, me; kings and queens, priestesses and warriors,
the river washes us away and who will remember us in the
unknown world that comes?
The holy men of the White Christ say we live forever,
with up their god in the sky somewhere – but they are fools
and worse, liars; I know the Mystery, I know the only truth
that matters, told me by an old woman, who was told it
by an old woman and every woman knows it in her heart:

As I am, so will you be;
As I am, so will you be...

I killed Grendel, I killed the only man I could have
truly loved; I brought Beowulf to Heorot, because of my
injured pride and he killed both my love and I
with his god-kissed iron blade and his restless, ruined spirit...

And that, for all it matters in the end, is the truth of it.

Love

Have you ever loved someone? I mean really loved them; loved them so much that you feel your heart would burst out of your body with it, and every drop of blood in you dances and glitters like the sun on water?

That's how I loved him. That's how I felt about him from the moment I was old enough to think of love. He'd been my dadda's apprentice, I'd known him all my life, so you'd think I'd have seen him as an uncle or something, but I didn't – I looked into his eyes that sweet, spring day and I knew he was the man I wanted.

Oh, at first, he was nervous – I mean I was so young, not quite fifteen; but he didn't resist for long. *My little girl*, he'd call me, *my precious little girl*. He was married of course, but his wife was a bitter stick of a woman with a haggard face and sharp, nagging tongue. He said she didn't understand him, that there was nothing between them. Of course I believed him and I never gave her a second thought when I clung to him in our secret hideaway. Now I'm an old woman with life's lessons stored up like winter grain in my heart, I know why she was so harsh; a strong woman chained to a weak man.

Because he was weak, and wicked. Not that it made me love him less; *the heart don't follow the head*, as my granny used to say. *The worse they are, the better we love 'em*, she'd cackle. When my body started to bloom with child, I found out quick enough how spineless he was, as he begged me, tears in his eyes, not to tell, not to ruin him... As if I wasn't ruined, pregnant at sixteen and from the most religious family in the village.

I couldn't hide it for long. My parents might have been overly devout but they weren't blind. They'd been older than was usual when they'd had me, their only child, and my mum always told everyone I was the gift of God; as if it was a personal thing between her and the Lord, a special reward for her piety. My dadda doted on me, I was his princess, his blessing, the comfort of his old age. His face was terrible to see when my mum dragged me weeping in front of him, screaming that I'd dishonoured us all, brought disgrace on the family, that she'd never be able to hold her head up in the village again. They demanded to know the man's name, but I felt love making bones and flesh in my belly and I said nothing.

They tried everything to find out; in the end, they brought the priest to me. He was a fool, the whole village thought it, but he was a priest and the only one we'd be likely to get, stuck out here in the sticks. He prayed with me, hour after hour, kneeling on the hard floor, his eyes squeezed shut, his waxy indoor face straining to contact the Lord until I nearly fainted with fatigue.

Tell me his name, he hissed at me over and over. *Tell me the sinner's name.* I thought I'd go mad with him and my folks yammering, pleading and shouting at me, hour after hour, day after day and then suddenly, I just couldn't stand it any more.

It was God, I said. *God gave me this child.* I meant, it was the gift of God, like my mum had always said of me. That was all. That was all, I swear. I never meant to deceive anyone; but it was too late. Their eyes grew round and the priest looked stern.

If this is a lie, you'll suffer for it, child; do not dare take the Lord's name in vain, he said.

I tried to explain, but the more I said, the worse it became and anyway, I saw hope, a dreadful kind of hope in my parent's eyes. If I was carrying the child of God, not some village lad's bastard brat, then glory would come of it, instead of shame. It was the perfect way out and like drowning souls, they took hold and wouldn't let go. Their unblinking faith was infectious. It was a kind of madness, the whole village caught it and talked of nothing else all that winter. Even the priest, who should have known better, believed it in the end. He wrote to learned men from the city and they came to question me; in the face of their authority and power I was scared dumb and dared not raise my eyes. They stroked their beards, talked and talked and ate my mum out of house and home. Then they declared solemnly I was a good and virtuous girl, from a family known to be pillars of the faith, who had been chosen by God to be His vessel. I was the handmaiden of the Lord and they hoped I was suitably grateful.

That was that, then. I was not a whore after all, and my family's honour was saved. Plans were laid, a member of the congregation found to marry me and make it all respectable and everyone was happy.

Except me, my heart breaking for the man I loved so desperately and who had been so unworthy.

I wept for hours; trapped in their iron hard belief and my youth. I wept for myself, for my baby and for the man who joined in the charade as loudly as the rest and begged me with his eyes not to betray him. I turned away and thought only of my child, who would be mine and mine alone, who would love me unconditionally for ever, who would be my consolation.

My son, my son; he looked so like his father to me, I was amazed no-one else remarked on it. The same dark eyes, the same sweep of raven eyelashes, the same thick, shining fall of hair – his hands, his neck, the curve of his cheek... All the love I had for the father went then to the son, my lovely boy. No-one said a word about how I spoilt and coddled him, because he was so special; everyone could see that. When he turned out to be clever and quick at his books as well as handsome, no-one was surprised, it was how it should be. I hoped he'd be a priest, a teacher, anything seemed possible. I was so proud of him. I folded away my secret until I almost forgot it myself and half believed my lie, my unintended lie.

But as my boy grew to manhood, things changed. I came to realise he wanted much, much more than being a country priest or a village scholar. He had grand ambitions – and he was ashamed of me. It hurt, it really hurt, but what could I do? I couldn't tell him the truth, he was still too young, it would destroy him. So I let it go, said nothing and promised myself I'd tell him when he was older, wiser and more able to understand. Anyway, the fact was, I understood his feelings, however painful they were to me. I wasn't an elegant, well dressed woman, with a lovely smart home he could bring his new friends to. I was a working man's wife, I couldn't even read. My boy wanted city life, the world of learning and brilliant minds, he wanted to *be* somebody and to lead the people into a better future. He thought I was backwards, ignorant. He didn't know how I had contrived to protect him, and myself; he couldn't know the desperate lengths I'd been driven to. All he knew were the whispers that had wreathed around him like incense smoke all his life; that he'd been born special, that he wasn't like the rest of us.

But it was very hard for me, in those early days. I knew he was embarrassed if I turned up at the church school to fetch him home for his dinner, or later, waited for him while he was at one of his discussion groups. I'd stand outside the door listening to him talk, all the time thinking, *this man they all admire so much is my son.* I loved him, what else could I do but watch over him? I was frightened by his daring thoughts and high-flown ideas, I thought they would get him into trouble and I blamed myself bitterly for creating the whole, foolish mess in the first place. I just wanted to protect him, to keep him safe.

But I couldn't. Not in the end. He offended too many powerful people; he was arrogant and full of self-belief, he had no doubt, he talked about his 'destiny', his 'fate' like young men do, having no fear of dying. His followers egged him on, encouraging him to speak publicly, to put himself forward and I couldn't stop him. I thought about telling him the truth then, saying, *son, do you remember the tall man who lived in the old white house by the stream, well...* But I couldn't; I kept meaning to, kept putting it off, then in the end it was all so fast. He was had up in court for preaching revolution... And it was too late.

I thought it would kill me stone dead; the pain of birthing him was nothing, *nothing* to the agony of seeing my child suffer like that and then die so horribly, believing himself deserted. His friends took care of me, as best they could; those wild-eyed young people full of crazy notions and big dreams. Nowadays, thinking to comfort me, they tell me my boy's ideas will change the world. I nod and smile, cursing those ideas and wishing only to have him back; to stroke his hair, to kiss his sweet face and watch him sleep.

I sit quiet and remember him, these days. I think of him not as they do, speaking to the crowds in his grown strength and beauty, but as a baby crowing at the shafts of sunlight in the dust-hazed dim of the workshop, clapping his little hands with joy. I remember his laughter, his kisses, his pretty, childish ways. People come and ask me for my memories and I'm always happy to talk about my boy, but I'm amazed at the things they say he did, the magic tricks they credit him with. And those old stories of his conception – well, they grow more strange with every repetition. They talk now of a great archangel that came to me in a still, white flame and whispered in my ear and I fell pregnant from it's voice alone; silliest of all, they say I stayed a virgin, intact, throughout my time and even through the birth. Oh, only a man could have thought that up, really...

But I don't care, I don't care. I don't have the learning to dispute with those who tell me these things as if I hadn't been there, as if he hadn't been my child; or who come looking to see a queen and are disappointed when they find me in my dusty old black dress. None of them would believe the truth now anyway. They don't want the truth, they want to believe, like my parents did.

But I know what I meant to say, all those years ago; I've had time to get it straight in my mind. I wanted to say that in making my baby, I was creating a wonder, a miracle, because every child is the result of something more than just our own, small, imperfect selves. My son was the son of God because every child is, and every mother is a Goddess in this mystery... Every new mother feels astounded at what's happening to her and thinks no-one has ever felt like this before in the whole long history of the world. It's just human nature, woman's nature. But I was too young to explain, and my parents, God rest their souls, too foolish and too concerned with their good name, to listen.

Secrets are awful things, take my word for it. They hang round your neck like millstones, they break your back and crush your spirit and lies just spawn more lies, and more and more, until the truth is buried so deep under them no one can dig it out. I just hope my poor lad's followers don't go causing trouble, or stirring things up too much in his name. I'm a countrywoman, after all, I don't like change for change's sake.

All I wish for now is that his friends knew he was the child of love; of ordinary, human love, but a love so strong, so simple, it has kept me silent to the grave. I wish they understood, these lads that hero-worship my son, that he was the very shape, sound, smell and touch of love to me. I've tried to tell them and they always go, *yes, yes, he always told us to love one another, don't you worry, mother, we won't let him down.* I can see they don't truly comprehend – it's all clever talk and cold ideas to them. Theories. They think like the men who came from the city to question me, all those years ago.

But I know the truth. I know it blood and breath, heart and head – and something else; the years have taught me that the simplest truths are the hardest to really understand.

My son was love.

The Chicken Boy

Love made him; human, simple, the body's singing
and the blood's deafening thunderous pulse;
life beating at the door; life that burst like a crocus bud
unravelling in the cold white shawl of late snow.

Love made him but who his dadda was the sisters
would never say; binding shame with silence
in the close twist of the village; narrow houses
clenched tight under the lee of the soft, green hills.

Love hid him; the iron hard love of family and
honour bright; and fear hid him, too; fear of the
clacking voices and the Church, fear of separation
and the cruel, pounding terror of disgrace.

Love hid him in the stinking dark of the yard,
in the shed amongst the ammoniac panic of feathers,
the beady ratchet of jetty eyes and dull dirty beaks;
hide the love child, hide the bastard in with the hens.

Love hid him there for years and years until the
prying boys ran screaming from the monster they
found in the old spinsters' chicken house,
and their dadda told the priest and it was over.

Love hid him in the convent then; the love of God
manifest in the nun's duty to their bridegroom;
suffering the little children, taking in the waifs,
hiding the monster from the staring, shrieking world.

Love made him; and the woman who told me this tale
tried to love him when as a girl, he was in her care;
tried to love the crushed and twisted thing that
cawed and gulped with such an avian, unhuman voice.

Love made him: And love hid him, and love
let the girl weep for him in that cold place; showed her
what love could do in all its many terrible and beautiful shapes,
and her tears were his blessing; though he, of course, would never know.

Venus

Venus dresses to go out in sequins and glitter;
the satisfying nubbly texture of
bead embroidery on denim jeans,
pink flip-flops encrusted with rose glass jewels.
Like a fabled queen from a dead past
she anoints her slender limbs with lotions that
glisten on her bright satin skin like gold leaf,
she sprays great billowing clouds of perfume
that fill the tiny bathroom with choking
vapour and seep through the crack under the door.

And her mother yells:

Venus! Venus girl! What you doin' stinking the house up?'

Venus sighs elastically and rolls her dreaming amber eyes
as she curls and curls her eyelashes with mascara
that promises glamour and fatal beauty
for only five ninety-nine;
she outlines her lips – that fat bow of
soft flesh – in burgundy and colours her mouth iridescent plum,
she rouges her cheekbones with silver-shot coral.

Pausing, she checks the mirror; pouts and smacks a practice kiss
considering the deadly effect she will create at the bus stop,
the boys she will devastate, the hearts she longs to break, having
known no heartbreak yet herself.

Venus! Venus! You gonna be in there all the damn night?

Venus gels her springing curls gleaming flat
and knots them tight at the nape of her slim gazelle's neck;
she picks up her earrings with the flat of her
fingers since her high c-curve acrylic nails,
painted in Burberry check, make delicate tasks difficult
and squinting fiercely, slides the gold posts through the
tiny dark slits in her narrow earlobes.

The heavy, Byzantine creoles drag and swing
as she turns her head to admire the creation of herself
in the old spotted mirror her mother had as a wedding gift.

Venus! Venus you come out now, I need to be in there!

Venus, languid with inhaled perfume and sure of the long grace
of her body sways onto the landing and poses, dramatically,
in the chipped doorframe.

Venus, Venus, God Almighty girl, you so pretty, so so pretty...

Venus, carefully, kisses her mother on the cheek that once
was as fresh and supple as her own, then with her thumb
wipes the lipstick from her mother's round face and says:

Off out. Love you, mum, bye.

The night receives Venus while her mother, enveloped
in the chemical blossoms of her daughter's scent, sits on the edge
of the wobbly plastic bath and smiles and cries all at the same time.

Two-Lane's Orison

Well, the night was sulphur-black as the Devil's dark heart
and the bright killing rain shot down like icy bullets;
you could hear its scurry-flurry rackety music hit the dirty
windows in a wind-driven snap-crack symphony that beat
in a freezing funky counterpoint to the jaunty bang-up
tunes blurting from the noise-blown speakers of the
geriatric stereo cranked up to *way* past bedtime:
and if you watched real hard – which was all they
had to do – you could almost see the greasy window glass
ripple in circular vibrations like it was a dirty pool
someone just lobbed a stone into – oh out, out, out
those glassy chaos rings of delusion wavered
in the dingy shine of the streetlamp haze,
and Two-Lane feared his mind would go out with them
if he didn't move, if he didn't move, if he didn't *move*
from the greasy embrace of the sofa's sagging bosom
and find some occupation for his jittering,
jerking, nail-biting, cud-chewing soul.

So, Two-Lane flew past Jimmy in a flap-bat welter of
baggy denim strides and his cap on backwards like
some fake-gangsta actor fool in a Hollywood film
and Jimmy saw this come to pass, in a slo-mo frame-by-frame
that almost, but not quite, stirred him to want to
ask, in a hazy kind of half-arsed way,
what the phat fuck Two-Lane was doing disturbing the vibe
with his screechy scratchy chitterings about boots and cash:
Because if Jimmy wanted noise, and all this demented disturbing blur,
man – he'd have got a chick in to bright-batter him with
her mascara meltdowns and flower-sour perfume clouds
since then at least he'd have had some sweet surrender
to compensate him for this rackety run-around.
So he opened his mouth; He. Opened. His. Mouth...
But his tongue refused to budge from its red ribbed
churney paradise of spit and mint-less chuddy so he shut his
blistered lips again and watched Two-Lane exit, stage left.

Which was the last he ever saw of feckless, faithless Two-Lane,
or the jam jar rent horde, or the minging, manky microwave,
and in the whole of Bradford's unfair City, blasted by winter,
chilled as a whore's cold grasp no-one noticed Two-Lane,
blissed out and baby-faced, fall behind the sharp glitter frosty
tree-spiked shrubland down by the old Magistrate's Court
he knew like the back of his dirty teenage hand
and falling, rolling, tip into sleep and from sleep drift
warm and easy into the dark folds of a cold-killed dying.
There he was, smiling his freeze-eyed stoner's smile as what
ran through his veins ran him up and out, high above the dank
and dingy loveless town to see his grandma, and his little sis,
bright as only the dead can be, saying *hey-hey Two-Lane*,
hey-hey sonny and kissing him, kissing him safe and sweet
in a glow-soft and perfect no-place that made him sigh a long
shivering exhale and give up his raggety-taggle ghost like a good 'un.

Gone, gone: Two-Lane's gone and forgotten fast as a fast-food
dinner in a plastic-nasty red-and-yellow food-hutch by the
motorway that he never travelled, save when as a glue-crazy youngster,
daring as only a fool ever is, he jitterbugged across the blacktop
causing horns to blare in a panicked cacophony and red-faced reps
in company cars to curse him as a misbegotten gutter-rat.
That narrow escape earned him his life's moniker of Two-Lane,
the dancing tarmac dodger of the Big Estate;
But that was as far as he got, after that he stuck and never
left the City in all his quick-time sleight of hand scavenger's
blink-and-he's-gone existence; until his number came up and the
lights flashed on his own personal pin-ball – tilt, tilt and ta-ta, Two-Lane.

And yes, the night was indeed as black as the Devil's heart
but it was all polar star, Jack Frost and glassy-gleaming
when tinsel choc-ad angels, lovely as rosy-painted tele-girls
bore Two-Lane to his final floaty fairy-light Paradise because...

The Devil didn't get Two-Lane's soul that night nor will he ever do:
Only the wicked go straight to Hell and Two-Lane? Well, Two-Lane
wasn't bright enough for wickedness or old enough for sin.
Two-Lane was a sixteen-year old brain-fried fuck-up,
innocent as only those who have been led to believe they're

blood-bad scum can be, who deserves to cop a break this once at least,
while the Man who sold him his hot-shot ticket out,
and the Man who sold that Man the crunchy, skanky,
cut-with-only-god-knows-what corrupted caustic shit,
who was sold his poison stash by a Man who answers to another
Man who travels business class and wears whisper-perfect
hand-stitched Italian suits from Harvey Nics and who doesn't
raise his blank blue eyes to a Man near the top – but not quite there -
well, those men, oh, *those* men the Devil knows are his,
and patient goat-foot gent that he is, he waits his time
and lets our Two-Lane,

bless him,

fade.

Bon voyage, Two-Lane, bon voyage.

Bon voyage, Two-Lane, bon voyage.

Rainy Night In Bradford

Rainy nights suit cities best; the snakeskin mambo gleam
of wet tarmac sequinned-stitched with streetlights
and that golden alien spaceship glow of the drive-thru
MacDonalds up on Leeds Road by the big roundabout.
In the rain and dark, dusty town trees are gravid with water,
heavy and shining with pure chandelier drops
and the dog rose hedge by the closed down motor shop
is sweet and fluttering with simple pale pink blossoms.

I'm driving us round and round the B&Q car park
while I learn the push, grunt and shift of gears;
we're smoking a little, listening to savage icy clear music swelling
and falling on the stereo like breathing ocean waves crashing
on arctic strands and the big old car sweeps in circles
and we all laugh and, swapping drivers, set off home, warm
and spicy in the car, then this girl, this skinny little white girl all
lo-rise bootcuts, shortie jacket and winking crystal-set belly-bar,
her hair a dog-rough yellow bleached draggle,
her mascara a seeping tarry smear is on the pavement by the
McDonalds screaming; she's screaming as a big guy lifts
her off the floor by her arm and her white trainers kick and kick.
We stop and park up; we watch – two Chinese men from the food place
watch too, porcelain faces set and waiting, we're all waiting.

And she slaps the guy and he drops her – thud – like a sack of rubbish
and she screams at him, the words ripping like torn rags
the swearing, dull, blunt, repetitive punching through every phrase,
spit and snot flying from her face into the drizzle.

She claws at his sleeve, wailing and choking with rage
and he walks away so she kicks him hard in the back of the thigh.

He hits her efficiently, without conviction and turns away to get
in his taxi and she hits him again and he throws her bodily over the
hedge.

We move now; us and the Chinese men. We move fast and careful
to her as she lies behind the shrubs soaking wet, piss drunk, stoned
and crying in breathless wheezing gasps cursing and her eyes rolling
up like dead pearls in the greasy black soot of her spoilt eye-make-up;
we comfort her but she doesn't hear and one of the Chinese men wraps
her in his parka but she throws it off and kicks her heels rat-tat-tat
in the dirt like a toddler having a temper tantrum until she's sick.

We all look at each other and sigh.

We phone the coppers and they don't come but the big guy does
and she gets back into the taxi and they drive off.

Then she makes him stop and come back and she winds the
window down and says thanks, thanks ever so, and we say
no problem and we all shake our heads in despair and the
Chinese men go.

We have five more calls with the coppers doing follow up.

I think she was married to the taxi-guy.
No reason, it was just something in the
practised rhythm of their violence.
I'll never know the end of the story; but then,
we never really do, do we?

Sic Transit Gloria Mundi

We put six black plastic bin bags of stuff in that Rent-A-Rek transit van; that's what we took and we left another twelve or so or of rubbish in the house. We'd cleaned up, too – or at least done what we thought of as cleaning; though it's no good excuse, you'd have needed an industrial steam cleaner to shift the muck in that kitchen. And we left a note, taped to the spotted mirror in the front room:

Dear Mr. Suleiman,
We are very sorry to run away and not pay what we owe you for the rent.
One day we will come back and settle up, we promise.
Yours sincerely,
The tenants at no. 166.

And we set off in the middle of the night, an old transistor radio and tape deck wedged on the filthy dashboard, the rain smearing the windscreen as the wonky wiper jerked spastically across the glass and we put 'Babylon's Burning' on at full distort and we laughed and you floored the pedal until the engine howled.

Oh, man; running away from Bradford in the lost, gone and sadly, not forgotten 1980's. Running into the great spirit gold of the rising sun and the hot rush of cutting loose at last from the viscous, clinging mud of Small Town England; every weekday the dole and just enough coarse cheap food to keep you alive, every Saturday night the same round of drinking, fighting and dreaming, every Sunday a long smashed afternoon of everyone droning on about how shit it was and how if only they had the breaks, cha, just watch 'em, they'd be rock stars and axe heroes and Somebodies.

If they had the breaks, yeah. If some god on high did it all for them and made it all for them, they'd be off to London in a trice, because that, we all knew, was where everything was. That's where über-cool parties were a dazed haze of glitter-floating beautiful people with clothes from boutiques so hip even their names were a transgression, where even the lowliest shop-girl was such a counter-culture punkette pin-up she got her pic in Sounds and the streets were paved with cocaine and the gutters ran with Jack in a fumey vapour of sweet decadence; rich boy's piss, the blood of rock n' roll. We all knew this to be one hundred and ten percent true because what journalist ever wrote paeans to the punk night at Queen's Hall, Bradford, or eulogies to some darktime niterie in say, oh, Chester? No, it was London; everything, everyone, every luminous, lush and longed-for treat was stashed in the belly of that old beast. It was a fact. We'd read it in every newspaper, Sunday arts supplement, music journal and fashionable novel since forever. It was the way it was and we were the huddled peasant masses crouching on our savage hills gazing up in the torch-lit dark at the divine superstar that was London, London, London.

So we sat in the van as it hurtled down the M1, wired out of our skulls with adrenaline and burning with Messianic passion white hot and calamitous. We weren't kids, oh no; we weren't teen escapees, you see; we were genuine artists, gone twenty-five and *almost* possessing a record contract with EMI; cash-poor we might be, but we'd worked like dogs and earned our turn at the table – so no pallid, plump, dumb fuck of a corporate recording executive was going to ruin our Big Chance. We would be there in the thick of it, in London, in control. We weren't going to be throwaway tinsel two-bit popstrels, oh no – we were going to change the face of music, of literature, of art, of life *forever*. Those decadent, air-and-arse kissing Londoners would be forced to welcome us with open arms because we were the future, we were the Warriors Of The New; strapped into our armour of hand-stitched leather and raggetty black we looked in my tattered old tarot cards and saw rapture rising behind us like a prophecy.

It had to be that way. We'd told everyone it would be. We'd been princes and princesses in Wooltown, now we were going to live like kings and queens in the Big Smoke. We'd chanted the spell, we'd invoked the gods. It was a done deal.

All that winter six of us slept on the spare bedroom floor of our singer's sister's shoe-box flat in the Northerner's ghetto of London, Highbury New Park. Done up like chrysalides in our stinking doss-bags we waited for Spring when we'd be turned into butterflies. At night the floor heaved like a living carpet and the air was sucked clean of oxygen, but it was too cold and grimy to open the window.

They'd never said how tumble-down, litter-strewn and dirty London was in those magazines and on the telly; the muck was terrible. Put on a clean T-shirt and it'd be black-bright in ten minutes of being exposed to the exhaust-fume leaden reek of the monstrous crawling traffic. Blow your nose and the snot was black; clean your make-up off and the grease was shot with gritty grey that wasn't mascara. The dirt had its own smell, too; sour and rank, hanging in the unmoving air like a filthy veil.

Back home, we'd think, each to ourselves and not letting on for fear of being thought soft, the cold, fresh wind off the moor unrolled through the canyons of gothic sandstone buildings, embroidered with the faint scent of heather and the sweet dust of the craglands, scouring the crooked streets and lighting wild roses in your cheeks.

But it was no use thinking like that. We were here to stay, to make our mark. So we'd shake ourselves back to the Now and think, hey – who cared about Wuthering Heights when we could go to Heaven, guest-listed on the strength of the last article in the NME about our meteoric rise to cult stardom, or my snarling mask adorning the front-cover of Time Out; Kabuki-style rebel-girl eyes sparking incandescent with unreason and fury. Fame, we thought, never having been taught to think otherwise, was better than bread – and infamy was preferable to anonymity. We didn't have to stand in line with the other runaways outside whatever night-club was in that week, listening to the chopped vowels and sing-song drawl of the North, the West or all the other great cities that netted the country; what Londoners called 'the Provinces' in that particular tone of voice that made you want to spit in their eye.

So we walked past the Liverpool whine or the Brummie choke of the queuing hordes, and strode in a cloud of patchouli, crimper-burnt hair and Elnett into the dreamland they could only hope for. A London night-club; wow. The carpets patinated with muck, spat-out gum and marinated in beer slops and puke. The glasses plastic and the watered-down drinks a fortune, the toilets a slick tsunami of bog-water and busted, stinking scrawled-on, paperless cubicles flapping with broken-locked doors. You never really got anything for nothing in London, see; proved how sharp they were, proved no-one got anything over on a real Londoner.

Not that we ever met a real Londoner. Not one born and bred, like. Maybe they were out there, somewhere, but we never found them. Certainly not one who could truly say they'd entered this vale of tears to the cheery clamour of Bow Bells, the coarse comforting din of the old pub pianner belting out 'Miybe It's Becorse I'm A Lannoner' and the smiles of Pearly Royalty handing out platters of jellied eels and cockles. No, folk said they were from London, but there was always somewhere else hidden in the dusty folds of their fast-forgotten past; they'd lived in London, oh, now, you know, God, forever. But they came from Leicester, or Bristol, or Glasgow or Cyprus or Athens, or Berlin or Ankara. They came to be famous, but until that bright day they washed dishes, threw plates of greasy nosh about in caffs or struggled round the heart-and-soul breaking savagery of the infamously brutal London dole offices.

Oh aye, it was a cold coming we, and many like us, had and no mistake. But what did we care? If we felt heartsick or homesick, we stood ourselves up straight, wiped our eyes if we were girls, unset our rock-hard jaws if we were boys and commenced afresh our sure-to-be stellar careers in the world of art. We would show them, we would not be broken and crawl off home like yellow, sag-bellied curs – we had a meeting with EMI tomorrow where we'd tell 'em how it was and tonight there was a Happening at an old warehouse by the river, promising an installation featuring a naked model-girl embedded in a tank full of jelly created by the latest cutting-edge performance art duo, a clutch of ranting skin-punk poets and a couple of hot new London bands cobbled together from the tatterdemalion remnants of last year's hot new London bands.

How many of those Happenings did we go to, expecting the dark whirligig of cruelly brilliant excess and getting instead a half-cocked mock-up in a rickety-rackety draughty squat where some anorexic pilled-up slapper was toted round in a rusty wheelbarrow slopping with lime Chivers by two public school-boys whose aristo Bo-Ho dads had been Hampstead artists in the 60's and people we recognised from magazines cooed about authenticity and artistic daring as they wiped their coke-snotty noses and patted each other on the back? They always, always all knew each other from school and from their families and they didn't know us – but suffering Jesus, we knew them – because we knew what real really was and they. Did. Not. Still don't, as it goes. Anyway, all these evenings ended in fighting, in smack and thunder brawls driven by our frustration and our rage at those whited sepulchres and their great stitch-up. How we frightened them, the faux-Londoners, how we shook their skinny trees. Yeah, yeah, yeah – all that talk of voyeuristic ultra-violence and the thrill of the street evaporated like oily vapour off a stagnant pond when they saw the lightening we were. They never knew us, no, they never did. They never saw us weep.

Oh, it was all such a shill, a sell, a sham; while we ripped ourselves apart searching for the pure, beating heart of things, believing we could, by telling the truth, by tearing the old lies apart at the seams, set ourselves and all our tribe free, London rolled on, a tottering juggernaut of blind and desperate delusion, all the little mannequins trying to find the tailor who made the Emperor's bee-yoo-ti-ful new clothes, so they could ape the great Cockalorum and maybe, maybe grab a tiny bit of reflected glory. It was a non-stop *danse macabre* and we didn't realise how bone-tired we were becoming.

Then, for us, it all came down in twenty-four hours.

First, we woke up and knew that yet again, we wouldn't be able to see the sky. Might not sound like much but it finally got to us, hemmed in and over-shadowed as we were by the ugly grey buildings crouching over us, the exhalations of air-cons and extractor fans panting rancid fast-food-farts into the starving air, choking us. In Bradford, you see, the skies constantly scroll above us in a massive cloudscape, as free and ever changing as the wild pulse of nature – the sandstone of the city is buttery amber, lit from within by a million prisms when the light hits it at sunset. We live in a flame, in a painting by Turner, in Gaia's Lamp. In London, we were dying for lack of light.

That morning, well, we knew it would be another London day, and lo! It was. And that night, it was my thirtieth birthday, and I wasn't a kid anymore. I had decided to have a party. It was to be at the Embassy Club, private, just for the tribe, and it would be a suitable send off to my dishevelled youth. I spent hours with the crimpers and the kohl-pot and I looked like the priestess at Knossos, but I covered up my breasts out of modesty. The snakes, well, I had them tattooed on; easier that way.

How long did my birthday party last in that tatty mould-smelling red velvet cellar before the scavenging liggers arrived, cawing over the booze they stole, screeching and cackling at us, the barbarians? How long was it before one of them abused the wrong soldier in our little army, and bang-bang it went? Not long, believe me. Then there were cracked noses, plum-black eyes, split lips swelling fat in an instant over sharp chipped teeth and the shrill screams of speed-skinny harridans egging on their leathery men-folk to try and 'fuck that bitch up'. That bitch stood as the maelstrom rolled around her in a sparkle of broken glass and the red stitch of blood and thought, ah, *enough*. So that bitch – which was me of course, naturally – picked up a tall bar stool and raising it overhead, smashed the great mirror by the bar into a blossom of shards so I wouldn't have to see my reflection backdropped by that screeching mess.

Then it went quiet, and all you could hear was breathing and a fella coughing where he'd been whacked in the gut. And the mangy jackels slunk off as the bouncers – late as ever – bulked into the room and tried to get leary and failed, no-one having the energy left to take them seriously.

And I went to the bar manager and said I was sorry for breaking his expensive looking-glass and he said I hadn't.

So I said – no, it was me, I'll pay for it, fair's fair, somewhat nervous though, as I was mortally skint as usual.

And he said, no, it wasn't you. But it was, I said. It was.

No, he said, it wasn't, you didn't do it, it's nothing; you're famous, we all know you, *people like you don't have to pay for what you do.*

And an abyss opened up in front of me that reeked sulphurous of what I could become, of what was in me that rubbed its corrupted hands together and murmured about fame, power and hubris, that would be the end of freedom and the death of my spirit and I knew too that a million wannabes would think me the biggest fool living for not pricking my thumb pronto and signing on the dotted line. So I threw some money on the bar – without doubt not enough – and walked out of that shabby shithole, my pretty golden boot-clogs crunching the broken mirror-glass and I felt a great disgust at the sorry, sordid smallness of the sell-out offered me. For if I was going to trade my immortal soul, brothers and sisters, would it be for the entree to crap clubs and pathetic parties in a slutty run-down frazzle of a city in a small island off the coast of Europe? Oh, I think not, I really think not, as it goes. Only the Universe would be enough to satisfy *my* desire, and I'm still working on that.

So we left London and returned to Bradford double-quick before we had time to think too hard. We rented another stone house terraced on the slopes of our crazy secret city's hills and breathed the good air with profound relief and paid Mr. Suleiman what we owed, and more, and he said he knew we'd come back one day and we all shook hands, straight up. Then we set ourselves to write our own histories in songs and stories, make our own testaments in paintings and books, which we have done and are still doing and will do for ever and ever, amen; stronger and stronger, brighter and brighter. And I'm grateful I saw what I saw when I did, before I was blinded by habit and despair, like so many I know who are lost now, beyond recall.

Twenty years have past since that night, and I ask myself what it really was we all hated most about our sojourn in the Great Wen. What was the grit in the pearl in the oyster, the time-bomb ticking heart of it. I've heard all the stories of loneliness and fear, of self-harm and suicide, of madness and addiction from others who finally limped home to lick their wounds – but it wasn't any of that, for us. No. What finally, finally finished us with London wasn't the corruption or the scandals, nothing so interesting, nothing so bold, nothing so grand.

Sic transit gloria mundi; so passes away the glory of the world.

London, that braggart capital, passes away without glory, you see. Without greatness, without any kind of joy, without passion or fire or beauty. In the end, you see, London was such a pathetic bloody *disappointment*.

And you know what? It still is.

That's all.

Winter and the City

It's a long slow courtship; played out every year
in the wet red fire of Autumn – a lingering flirtation,
the filigree flounce of amber leaves skirling round dark alleys;
then a sudden cold snap; followed by a forgiving day so warm
old cats stretch in the sun's pockets dreaming of feral loves long past.

Then things proceed in earnest; one morning I hear my neighbour
cursing in clouds of vapour as his work boots slip on
frost granulated over slippery green flagstones;
a sharp salty rime glitters on the skinny rose bushes;
they look like elderly duchesses with their diamond tiaras askew.

And one day, the high wild skies are shrouded
with cloud blinds that filter a strange aquatic light,
like the cool glow of saltwater pulsing sluggishly under
ocean ice-caps; the cats shiver like dandies in their silks
and won't hazard the raw, perishing garden.

The snow is coming; I snuff the air in a blind instinct
for the smell of it, gravid on the still air, iron damp.
Huddled in quilts I dream of wedding cakes,
tier on tier of stiff sugar sculpture whiter than old bone,
whiter than my grandmother's pearls, and just as chill.

Next morning, I wake, blood thick and slow with ice slush,
to find beautiful new snow wreathing the drooping trees;
the streets freshly powdered and polar bright; everything mantled
and veiled with the alabaster bridal lace that's brought out every year
for the day when Winter marries the City again.

So Many Names Are Lost Now

Commissioned by The Royal Armouries, Leeds and dedicated to Captain
Ronald Mumford

So many names are lost now; war-tilled fields of clotted poppies
waltz in ragged scarlet, blown by the breath of winds that carry a cruel
dust of bone; on far mountains, relics, stony as saints, lie silent under
vestments of snow; in white deserts, furnace-bright and inexorable,
empty ivory cages are all that remain of men who moved in those bodies,
in those earth-returning remnants; eyes, now still and sky-turned,
saw wonders, saw their children; saw love, friendship and desire; saw the
seasons' long fertile turning; they witnessed the swift brute tangle
of combat; the sickening lurch of fear and smelt the coppery stink
of bright blood springing from other men they had learnt to call the
                                                                    enemy.

So many forms of warfare: the battle roiling with screams and the sky
above embroidered with the swift dark economy of carrion birds;
the tension of sieges, creaking with battering engines, the notched arrow
straining to leap ecstatic from the long bow, the sword named
                                                    Widowmaker,
the great insect carapace of plate armour, the grim click of a rifle cocked,
the ratchet lurching dance of tanks, the trench soaked in mud and misery
that only poets knew the broken heart of, the sky ripped with tracer fire,
and the bomb; brutal, consuming – the vast, shocking detonation,
or a device, bound to the fanatic body of a child unable to understand what
death really is and how no god, but man, called them to that sacrifice.

So many memorials to our wars; we house its machines in bright halls and
wonder at their cruel beauty as they hang waiting for their time to
                                                    come again,
but we forget the actuality of the lives these savage instruments took.
The dead cannot speak, cannot plead with us while the receding
waves of weeping fade and they dwindle into the dark despite
the ranks of crosses, the triumphal arches, the eternal flames.
Oh, all those boys, all those dead boys; how can we forget them?
How can we call them brutes or fools and turn away because we are
afraid to look at what they did, in case we see it in ourselves?
Read the names and call them home; chant a litany of remembrance.

So many lessons we never learnt; these dead should be our teachers, they are the true witnesses, only they know the horror and the ever repeating failure that is war; the sickness we return to generation after generation because we fail to hear the testament of those who were sacrificed to pride, to greed or to ideology – let the battlefield dead take our hands in theirs and illuminate in the sweet blue twilight of our memories the most precious truth we can ever learn – let there be peace; learn this if nothing else: Let there be peace – listen, can't you hear their voices clamouring in a thousand tongues – let there be peace for all of us and let all the fallen, all of them, truly rest in peace at last.

Read the names and call them home; chant a litany of remembrance.
Read the names and call them home.
Read the names and call them home.
Read the names – and call them home.

The Ribbon

In 1926 the Royal Tombs of Ur were dug up by an Englishman with a title and the time to do such a thing; time to get the money for an expedition to the flood-washed plains; time to set up his canvas city and stare out at the burnt dusty land while the sing-song babble of his workers rose and fell like the twin rivers he gazed at.

The tombs were elaborate, bursting with treasure; harps and chariots, jewellery and statues; lapis-lazuli, carnelian, silver, cedar and white shell. And bodies, layer upon layer of bodies; the Great King and all his warriors, grooms and courtiers, the Queen Shub-ad with her musicians and her ladies, all the court women laid in neat rows. Sixty-eight women, as if asleep.

They wore their most intricate costumes, beaded, with red cloaks and shell-ring belts, their twisted hair braided with gold or silver ribbons; all identical down to the enormous half-moon earrings and the necklaces threaded from blue and gold, strand after strand reaching down their breasts like a waterfall, still and frozen by death and time.

Except one woman. She lay more awkwardly and her hair was not tied with a ribbon like the others; she was young, as far as could be told and her ribbon was still rolled, like a child's before the party, in her pocket. She had been late, it would seem; late to the ceremony that would allow her to faithfully accompany her Queen into the next life, late for the sleeping drug or the poisoned cup that would free her soul.

And I wonder; did she run through the painted corridors of the palace, her red cloak billowing out behind her, her sandalled feet like white doves flying, tears of vexation shining on her round face? Had she said goodbye to her lover one last time, promising they'd meet again, she knew they'd meet again and one last, one last sweet kiss tasting of honey and salt? Had she just overslept because she'd spent her last night frightened and alone with no-one to confess her terror to? Or was she just the sort of girl who means to be on time but never is, flinging on her jewellery, stuffing her ribbon in her pocket, running and fastening up her dress; catching at her cloak, scolding herself as she tripped and breathless saw the cross faces of the priests who waited for her, and her friends' exasperated glances, dark eyes gleaming from the dull black bands of kohl – late, even for this.

She drank the cup, her heart still beating quickly, her little face flushed and pink and she went with her Queen into death. Lying still, undisturbed, resting at last in the long night until the Englishman and his workers dug her from the earth and found her ribbon, still rolled, the ends of the silver cloth tucked under so it wouldn't come undone.

Wedding Song

And underneath it all, two hands clasped:
Beyond the ritual and the words spoken,
out of time and the endless turning of the days.
Each to each.

Each to comfort each, gentle against the high solitude
of life and the racing blood of it,
each to be kind to each, without thinking, reflexive –
the small love that is transcendent.
Each to be a shield burnished and bright
for the other, against the fury
that beats within and the great unknowable
stretching fearfully before.

And underneath it all, underneath it all
now and without ending,
all it means, *all*, perfect and true
in the moment and the years,

two hands clasped and the lover's kiss,

two hands clasped.